# COGAT®
# GRADE 3
# MATH

## 3 Practice Tests
## Level 9

Savant Test Prep™

www.SavantPrep.com

## Please leave a review for this book!

Thank you for purchasing this resource.

Please take a moment to leave a
review on the website where you purchased this.

# TABLE OF CONTENTS

## INTRODUCTION

COGAT® General Information ................................................................. 4

How To Use This Book .......................................................................... 5

Test-Taking Tips .................................................................................... 5

Question Examples ............................................................................... 6

## PRACTICE TEST 1 (WORKBOOK FORMAT)

Number Puzzles ..................................................................................... 11

Number Series ....................................................................................... 15

Number Analogies ................................................................................. 20

## PRACTICE TEST 2

Number Puzzles ..................................................................................... 26

Number Series ....................................................................................... 30

Number Analogies ................................................................................. 34

## PRACTICE TEST 3

Number Puzzles ..................................................................................... 39

Number Series ....................................................................................... 43

Number Analogies ................................................................................. 47

## ANSWER KEYS

Answer Key for Practice Test 1 (Workbook Format).............................. 52

Answer Key for Practice Test 2 ............................................................ 54

Answer Key for Practice Test 3 ............................................................ 56

ADDITIONAL BOOK INFORMATION................................................... 57

# INTRODUCTION

## COGAT® GENERAL INFORMATION

- COGAT® stands for Cognitive Abilities Test®.
- The test measures students' reasoning skills and problem-solving skills.
- It provides educators with an overall assessment of students' academic strengths and weaknesses.
- The COGAT® is commonly used as a screener for gifted and talented programs.
    - Gifted and Talented (G&T) selection sometimes requires a teacher recommendation as well.
- The test is usually administered in a group setting.
- A teacher (or other school associate) administers the test, reading the directions.
- Please check with your school/testing site regarding its testing procedures, as these may differ.

## COGAT® LEVEL 9 FORMAT

- Students in third grade take the COGAT® Level 9.
- The Quantitative (Math) Battery has 52 questions.
- The test is divided into 3 main parts, each called a "Battery." Each Battery has three question types. See the chart below.

| VERBAL BATTERY | NON-VERBAL BATTERY | QUANTITATIVE BATTERY |
|---|---|---|
| Verbal Analogies: 22 Questions | Figure Analogies: 20 Questions | Number Puzzles: 16 Questions |
| Verbal Classification: 20 Questions | Figure Classification: 20 Questions | Number Series: 18 Questions |
| Sentence Completion: 20 Questions | Paper Folding: 16 Questions | Number Analogies: 18 Questions |

- Often, schools administer one Battery per day, allowing approximately 45 minutes per Battery.
- Students have around 15 minutes to complete each question type (for example, students would have around 15 minutes to complete Verbal Analogies).
- See the following pages for examples and explanations of each question type.

## COGAT® SCORING

- Students receive points for correct answers. Points are not deducted for incorrect answers. (Therefore, students should at least guess versus leaving a question blank.)
- In general, schools have a "cut-off" COGAT® score, which they consider together with additional criteria, for gifted & talented acceptance. This varies by school.
- This score is usually at least 98%. (However, some schools accept scores of 95% or even 85%.)
- A score of 98% means that your child scored as well as, or better than, 98% of those in his/her testing group.
- COGAT® scores are available for the entire test and can be broken down by Battery.
- Depending on the school/program, such a "cut-off" score may only be required on one or two of the Batteries (and not on the test overall).
- It is essential to check with your school/program for their acceptance procedures.
- The COGAT® Practice Tests in this book can not yield these percentiles because they have not been given to a large enough group of students to produce an accurate comparison/calculation.

# HOW TO USE THIS BOOK

1. Go over the Question Examples together with your child. These begin on the next page.

2. Do Practice Test 1 (Workbook Format)
   - Do these questions with your child, especially if this is your child's first exposure to COGAT®-prep questions. These questions have a "workbook format," meaning they are meant to be done together.
   - Do not assign a time limit.
   - Talk about what the question is asking your child to do.
   - Questions progress in difficulty. (The first few questions are quite simple.)
   - Go over the answers using the Answer Key.
   - For questions missed, go over the answers again, discussing what makes the correct answer better than the other choices.

3. Do the remaining Practice Tests following Practice Test 1.
   - If your child progressed easily through Practice Test 1, see how well they can do without your help.
   - If your child needed assistance with much of Practice Test 1, then continue to assist your child with Practice Test 2.
   - If you wish to assign a time limit, assign around 15 minutes per question type.
   - Go over the answers using the Answer Key.
   - For questions missed, go over the answers again, discussing what makes the correct answer better than the other choices.

4. **Need more practice?**

   - **Get 300+ new questions per book.**

   - **Check out Savant Test Prep™ books on Amazon®.**

# TEST-TAKING TIPS

- Ensure your child listens carefully to the directions, especially in the Sentence Completion section.
- Make sure (s)he does not rush through questions. (There is no prize for finishing first!) Tell your child to look carefully at the question. Then, tell your child to look at each answer choice before marking his/her answer.
  - If you notice your child continuing to rush through the questions, tell him/her to point to each part of the question. Then, point to each answer choice.
- If (s)he does not know the answer, then use the process of elimination. Cross out any answer choices which are clearly incorrect, then choose from those remaining.
- This tip/suggestion is entirely at your discretion. You may wish to offer some sort of special motivation to encourage your child to do his/her best. An extra incentive of, for example, an art set, a building block set, or a special outing can go a long way in motivating young learners!
- The night before testing, it is imperative that children have enough sleep, without any interruptions. (Think about the difference in **your** brain function with a good night's sleep vs. without. The same goes for your child's brain function.)
- The morning before the test, ensure your child eats a healthy breakfast with protein and complex carbs. Do not let them eat sugar, chocolate, etc.
- If you can choose the time your child will take the test (for example, if (s)he will take the test individually, instead of at school with a group), opt for a morning testing session, when your child will be most alert.

# QUESTION EXAMPLES

- Here is an overview of the COGAT® question types.
- This section has simple examples, to introduce your child to test concepts.
    - Do these examples together with your child.
- Below the questions are explanations for parents.

## 1. NUMBER PUZZLES (QUANTITATIVE BATTERY)

• **Directions:** Which number would be in place of the question mark so that both sides of the equal sign are the same?

• **Explanation:** These questions have two formats. The first example is a standard math problem. In the second example, your child needs to replace the black shape with the given number. Should your child have problems figuring out the answer of either format, (s)he can simply test each answer choice until they find the correct answer. The answer to #1 is E. The answer to #2 is D.

1. $19 = ? + 5$      A. 5     B. 24     C. 20     D. 4     E. 14

2. $? = \blacklozenge - 8$      A. 0     B. 1     C. 2     D. 3     E. 4
   $\blacklozenge = 11$

## 2A. NUMBER SERIES (QUANTITATIVE BATTERY), TEXT FORMAT

• **Directions (read to child):** The top row of numbers have made a pattern. Which answer choice would complete the pattern?

• **Number Format Explanation:** To help your child see the pattern, ask them to write the difference between each number and the next. Here, the difference between 6 and 9 is 3. The difference between 9 and 12 is 3. The difference between 12 and 15 is 3, and so on. In less challenging questions, this "difference" will be the same for each set of numbers. If the pattern is "add 3," then the answer is 21, because 18 +3 = 21.

| 6 | 9 | 12 | 15 | 18 | ? |
|---|---|----|----|----|---|

A. 21     B. 3     C. 22     D. 24     E. 30

In more challenging questions, this pattern is not consistent with each set of numbers. See below:

| 30 | 29 | 27 | 24 | 20 | 15 | ? | Pattern: -1, -2, -3, -4, etc.; Answer: 9 |
|----|----|----|----|----|----|---|----|

| 7 | 2 | 1 | 7 | 2 | 1 | ? | Pattern: 7 - 2 - 1; Answer: 7 |
|---|---|---|---|---|---|---|----|

| 3 | 4 | 6 | 7 | 9 | 10 | ? | Pattern: +1, +2, +1, +2, etc; Answer: 12 |
|---|---|---|---|---|----|---|----|

| 5 | 0 | 6 | 0 | 7 | 0 | ? | Pattern: every other number +1; every other number = 0; Answer: 8 |
|---|---|---|---|---|---|---|----|

## 2B. NUMBER SERIES (QUANTITATIVE BATTERY), ABACUS FORMAT

• **Directions (read to child):** Which rod should go in the place of the missing rod to finish the pattern?

• **Explanation for #1 (read to child):** Before the missing rod, the other rods have made a pattern that we need to figure out. Then, we will complete the pattern with the correct answer choice. From left to right, we see that the pattern is: 1 - 2 - 1 - 2 - 1. After 1, comes 2. This means that the missing rod needs 2 beads.

• Make sure your child accurately counts the number of beads. In the examples below, there are numbers under the rods indicating the number of beads. The practice test questions do not have these numbers.

• After you do #1, go over questions #2 - #7 together. The pattern and the answer are already given.

1.

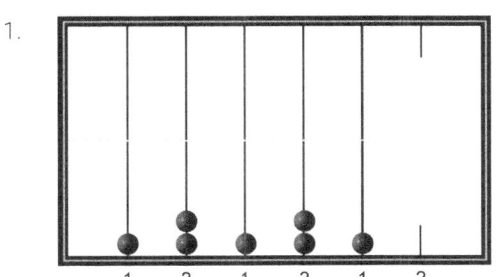 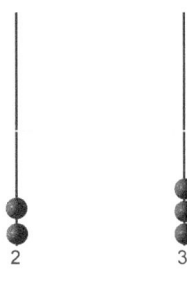

Pattern: the number of beads decreases by 1. The answer is 1.

2.

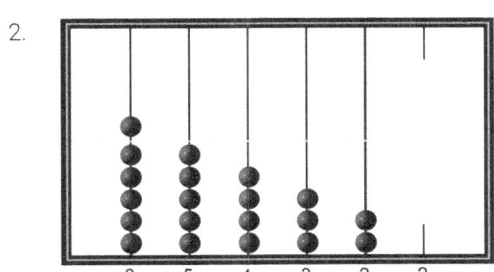 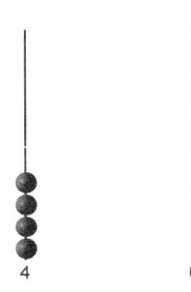

Pattern: every other rod increases by 1. And, the alternate rods equal 0. The answer is 0.

3.

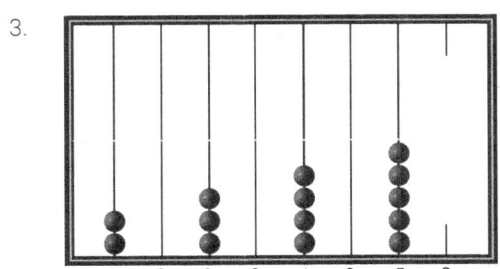 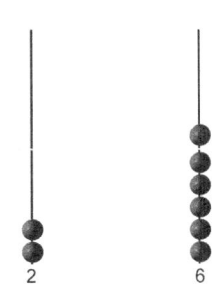

Pattern: the rods repeat 7 - 5 - 3. The answer is 7.

4.

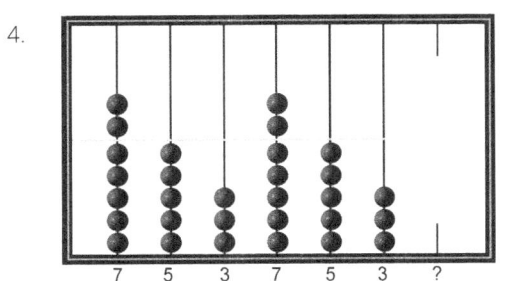 

7

Every other rod increases by one (1 - 2 - 3 - 4). Then, every other rod (the alternate rods), increases by one (4 - 5 - 6 - 7). With the alternating rods increasing 1, 2, 3, 4, this means that the next rod will be 5.

5.

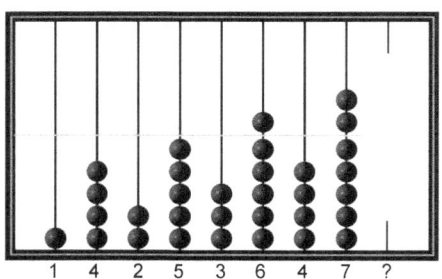  

Every other rod decreases by one (5 - 4 - 3). Then, every other rod (the alternate rods), increases by one (1 - 2 - 3). With the alternating rods decreasing 5, 4, 3, this means that the next rod will be 2.

6.

Pattern: the rods decrease with the pattern 6 - 4 - 2, then increase with the reverse pattern 2 - 4 - 6.

7.

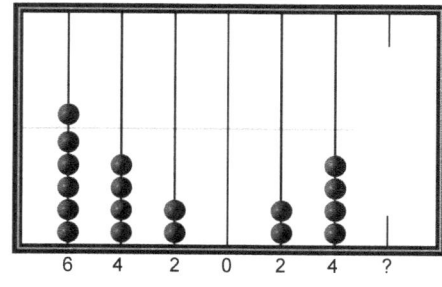  

## 3A. NUMBER ANALOGIES (QUANTITATIVE BATTERY), FORMAT 1

• **Directions:** Look at the first two sets of numbers. Come up with a rule that both of these sets follow. Use this rule to figure out which answer choice goes in place of the question mark in the last set of numbers.

• **Explanation (read to child):** Have your child figure out a rule that explains how the first number "changes" into the second number. It could use addition, subtraction, multiplication, or division. Have him/her write the rule by *each* pair. (S)he must make sure this rule works with *both* pairs. The rule for the first question is "+4," so 33 is the answer.

| 5 | → | 9 |

| 11 | → | 15 |

| 29 | → | ? |     A. 25    B. 33    C. 4    D. 24    E. 32

## 3B. NUMBER ANALOGIES (QUANTITATIVE BATTERY), FORMAT 2

• **Directions:** Look at the first two sets of numbers. Come up with a rule that both of these sets follow. Use this rule to figure out which answer choice goes in place of the question mark in the last set of numbers.

• **Explanation (read to child):** In the first set, it may appear that the rule is "add 4," because 2 + 4 = 6. However, looking at the second set, you see that this rule does not work. Let's go back to the first set. How else can you go from 2 to 6? You can multiply: 2 x 3 = 6. Let's try the rule "multiply by 3." Apply this rule to the second set: 4 x 3 = 12. The rule "multiply by 3" works in both sets. In the third set, 10 x 3 = 30 (choice D).

[2 → 6]     [4 → 12]     [10 → ?]     A. 6    B. 3    C. 13    D. 30    E. 7

---

Parents, read the below with your child.

Watch out!

This book is filled with tricky questions. Can you answer them?

Of course you can!

Pay close attention to each question and try your best.

We'll be here to help you along the way!

# COGAT® PRACTICE TEST 1
# (WORKBOOK FORMAT)

# NUMBER PUZZLES

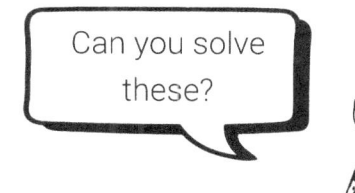

Sara

**Directions (read to child):** Look at the box that has the question mark. Which number would go here so that both of the sides of this equal sign (point to the equal sign) have the same amount?

**Additional information (for parents):** Be sure your child pays attention to the plus and minus signs. Some questions have two different signs. During the actual test, your child will most likely be able to use scratch paper. So, allow them to use scratch paper here if they wish. Page 6 has additional Number Puzzles tips.

**Example:** The left side of the equal sign has 12. Which answer choice do you need to put in place of the question mark so that the right side of the equal sign totals 12?

25 minus 13 equals 12. So, C is the correct answer.

1    **12  =  25  –  ?**

A  11        B  12        C  13        D  14        E  25

2    **18  +  21  =  50  –  ?**

A  9        B  10        C  11        D  12        E  13

**3**  **42  =  50  −  4  −  [ ? ]**

(A) 3          (B) 4          (C) 5          (D) 6          (E) 7

**4**  **30  =  45  −  20  +  [ ? ]**

(A) 8          (B) 7          (C) 6          (D) 5          (E) 4

**5**  **90  =  48  +  30  +  [ ? ]**

(A) 12          (B) 11          (C) 72          (D) 13          (E) 14

**6**  **80  −  16  =  70  −  [ ? ]**

(A) 4          (B) 64          (C) 10          (D) 12          (E) 6

**7**  **37  +  25  =  80  −  [ ? ]**

(A) 17          (B) 62          (C) 19          (D) 18          (E) 68

**8**

$$85 = 72 - 8 + \boxed{?}$$

A  5          B  20          C  16          D  22          E  21

**Note:** In the rest of the questions, your child will need to replace the black diamond with the given value to solve the problem.

**9**

$$\boxed{?} = \blacklozenge + 62$$
$$\blacklozenge = 19$$

A  70          B  81          C  72          D  73          E  74

**10**

$$\boxed{?} = \blacklozenge \times 5$$
$$\blacklozenge = 6$$

A  20          B  25          C  30          D  35          E  11

**11**

$$\boxed{?} = \blacklozenge \div 4$$
$$\blacklozenge = 16$$

A  4          B  3          C  6          D  5          E  12

**12**

$$\boxed{?} = \blacklozenge \times 7$$
$$\blacklozenge = 5$$

A  25          B  30          C  15          D  40          E  35

13

$$? = \blacklozenge \div 3$$
$$\blacklozenge = 27$$

(A) 27   (B) 7   (C) 8   (D) 9   (E) 24

14

$$? = \blacklozenge + 35 - 12$$
$$\blacklozenge = 20$$

(A) 38   (B) 39   (C) 40   (D) 41   (E) 43

15

$$? = \blacklozenge + 50 + 20$$
$$\blacklozenge = 8$$

(A) 78   (B) 69   (C) 70   (D) 71   (E) 38

16

$$? = \blacklozenge - 24 - 18$$
$$\blacklozenge = 75$$

(A) 30   (B) 31   (C) 32   (D) 33   (E) 34

Great job! Let's do some more!

Emma

# NUMBER SERIES

Kai

What goes in place of the missing rod?

**Directions (read to child):** Here, you must try to figure out a pattern that the numbers have made. Which answer choice would complete the pattern?

**Parent note:** Some questions are in the form of #1 (an abacus). Some are in the form of #8 (a series of numbers). Pages 6 and 7 have additional Number Series tips.

**Example #1:** Here is an abacus. The abacus rods have made a pattern: 0 beads, 7 beads, 0 beads, 5 beads, 0 beads, 3 beads, and 0 beads.

Here we see that every other rod has "0" beads. (The first, third, fifth, and seventh rods have 0.)

Also, every other rod (the second, fourth, and sixth rod) have two less beads each time.

If this is true, how many beads would the rod that is missing have? What is three take away 2? It's 1.

So, the rod with 1 bead is the answer.

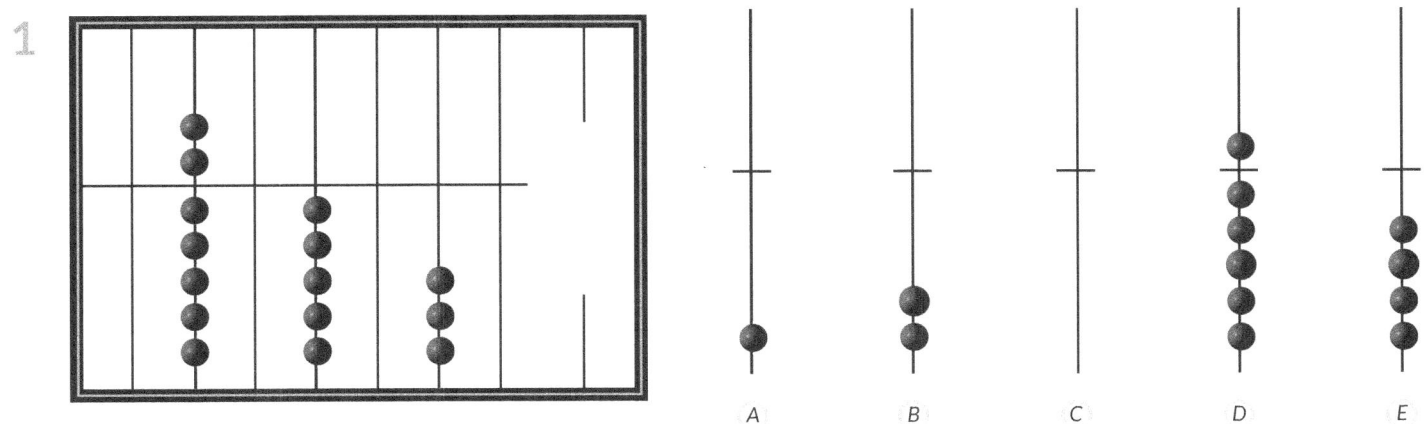

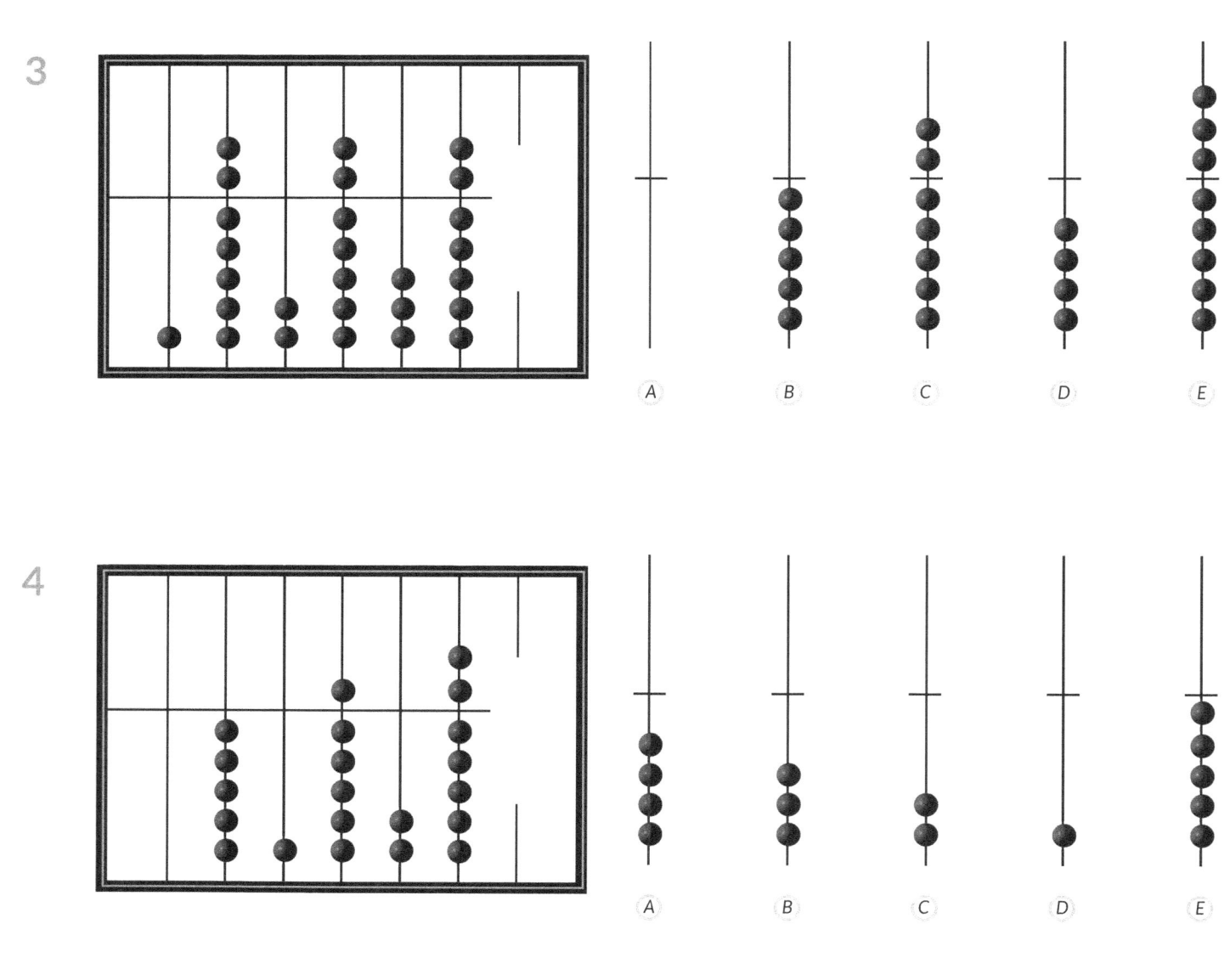

**5**

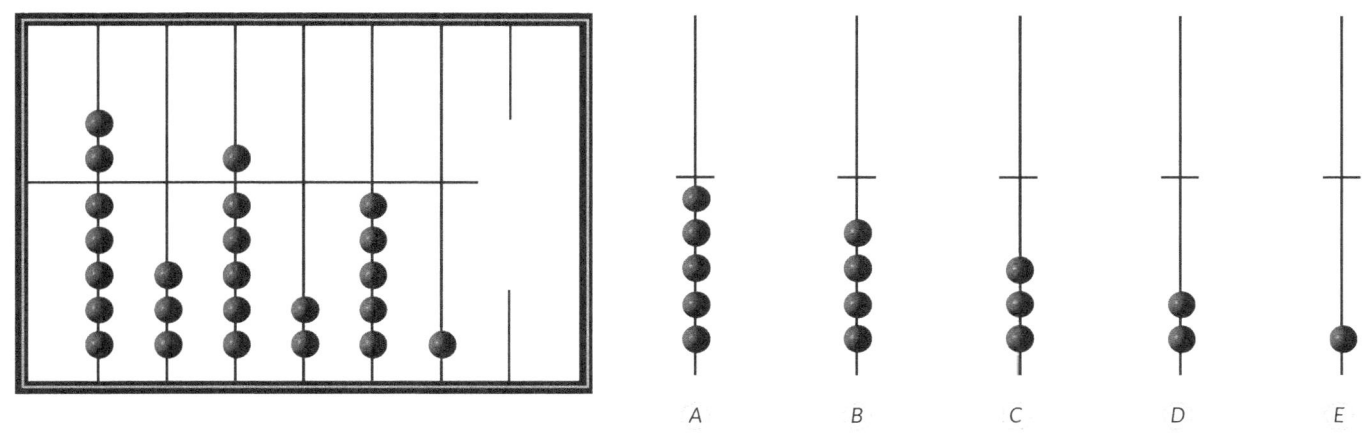

A    B    C    D    E

**6**

A    B    C    D    E

**7**

A    B    C    D    E

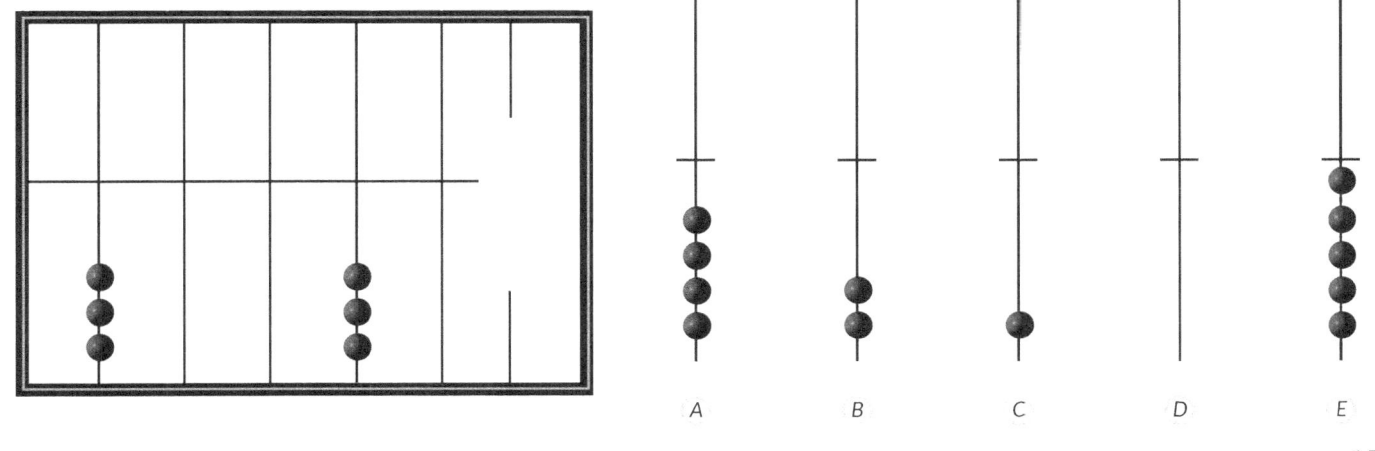

**8**  8    12    16    20    24    ?

(A) 26    (B) 27    (C) 28    (D) 29    (E) 30

**9**  3    4    6    7    9    10    ?

(A) 10    (B) 11    (C) 12    (D) 13    (E) 14

**10**  20    19    17    16    14    13    ?

(A) 13    (B) 11    (C) 10    (D) 12    (E) 8

**11**  5    7    10    12    15    17    ?

(A) 18    (B) 19    (C) 22    (D) 21    (E) 20

**12**  8    10    10    12    12    14    ?

(A) 14    (B) 15    (C) 16    (D) 17    (E) 18

**13**  20    19    18    16    15    14    12    ?

(A) 14    (B) 13    (C) 12    (D) 11    (E) 10

**14**   3.1   5.1   7.1   9.1   11.1   13.1   ?

A 14.1   B 18.1   C 17.1   D 16.1   E 15.1

**15**   35   42   49   56   63   70   ?

A 75   B 76   C 77   D 78   E 79

**16**   15   20   30   35   45   50   ?

A 55   B 56   C 57   D 58   E 60

**17**   49   60   54   65   59   70   ?

A 62   B 63   C 64   D 65   E 66

**18**   10   11   12   12   13   14   ?

A 14   B 15   C 16   D 17   E 18

**19**   25   23   24   22   23   21   ?

A 19   B 20   C 21   D 22   E 23

# NUMBER ANALOGIES

How do they all go together?

Maya

**Directions (read to child):** Look at the first two sets of numbers. Try to come up with a rule that both of these sets of numbers follow. Take this rule and try to figure out which answer choice goes in the place of the question mark to complete the third set of numbers.

**Parent note:** A more detailed explanation and a Number Analogies example question are on p.9. If you have not already, look over p.9.

Number Analogies questions are in two forms: the form of #1 (3 sets aligned vertically with boxes around the numbers) or in the form of #8 (3 sets aligned horizontally with no boxes).

**Example #1:** In the first set of numbers, we see 10 and 9.

In the second set, we see 7 and 6.

How would you get from 10 to 9? How would you get from 7 to 6?

In each, you take away 1 from the first number. This could be the "rule" that both sets follow.

Let's take this rule and apply it to the bottom set.

What is the answer when have 3, and then take away 1? The answer is 2.

1

| 10 | → | 9 |
| 7 | → | 6 |
| 3 | → | ? |

(A) 1          (B) 2          (C) 0          (D) 4          (E) 5

**2**

| 5 | → | 10 |
| 9 | → | 18 |
| 4 | → | ? |

A  5          B  6          C  8          D  9          E  13

**3**

| 40 | → | 43 |
| 22 | → | 25 |
| 18 | → | ? |

A  19          B  20          C  21          D  22          E  23

**4**

| 3 | → | 12 |
| 6 | → | 24 |
| 7 | → | ? |

A  28          B  30          C  32          D  4          E  11

**5**

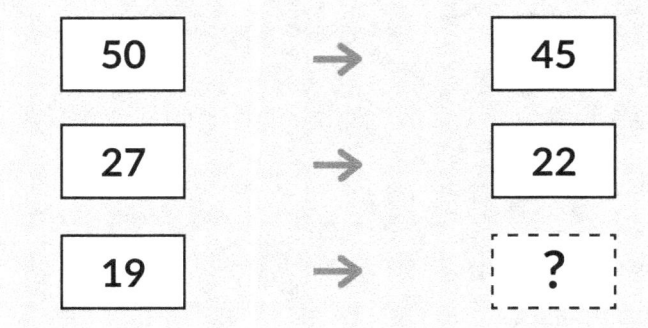

| | | |
|---|---|---|
| A | 24 | |
| B | 15 | |
| C | 12 | |
| D | 10 | |
| E | 14 | |

**6**

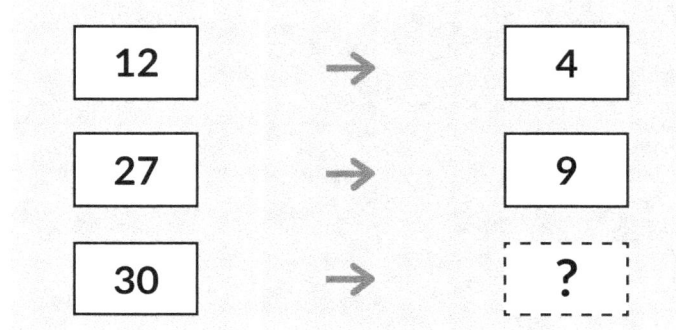

| | | |
|---|---|---|
| A | 22 | |
| B | 33 | |
| C | 27 | |
| D | 10 | |
| E | 12 | |

**7**

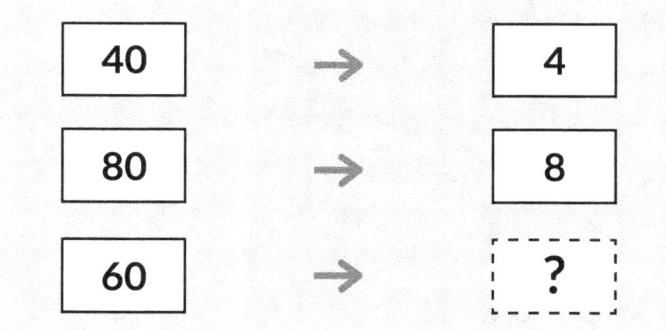

| | | |
|---|---|---|
| A | 6 | |
| B | 7 | |
| C | 8 | |
| D | 9 | |
| E | 10 | |

8    [33 → 42]    [31 → 40]    [29 → ?]

A 36        B 37        C 38        D 39        E 40


9    [12 → 6]    [20 → 10]    [16 → ?]

A 2        B 6        C 14        D 9        E 8


10    [42 → 34]    [52 → 44]    [62 → ?]

A 70        B 54        C 56        D 58        E 60


11    [44 → 38]    [33 → 27]    [55 → ?]

A 47        B 48        C 49        D 50        E 61


12    [8 → 16]    [47 → 55]    [30 → ?]

A 22        B 36        C 37        D 38        E 60

**13**   [12 → 0]        [22 → 10]        [34 → ?]

(A) 20        (B) 0        (C) 40        (D) 23        (E) 22

**14**   [3 → 18]        [5 → 30]        [6 → ?]

(A) 36        (B) 12        (C) 32        (D) 16        (E) 21

**15**   [24 → 14]        [20 → 10]        [12 → ?]

(A) 6        (B) 22        (C) 10        (D) 8        (E) 2

**16**   [40 → 10]        [36 → 9]        [32 → ?]

(A) 5        (B) 28        (C) 36        (D) 8        (E) 12

**17**   [60 → 53]        [14 → 7]        [54 → ?]

(A) 27        (B) 61        (C) 47        (D) 8        (E) 64

**18**   [30 → 10]        [21 → 7]        [18 → ?]

(A) 4        (B) 5        (C) 6        (D) 7        (E) 8

# COGAT® PRACTICE TEST 2

# NUMBER PUZZLES

**Directions:** Which number would go in place of the question mark so that both of sides of the equal sign (point to the equal sign) have the same amount?

**1**

$$70 = \boxed{?} + 45$$

A) 45  B) 25  C) 26  D) 27  E) 115

**2**

$$50 = 74 - \boxed{?}$$

A) 20  B) 124  C) 22  D) 23  E) 24

**3**

$$49 \div \boxed{?} = 7$$

A) 5  B) 6  C) 7  D) 8  E) 9

**4**

$$8 \times \boxed{?} = 48$$

A) 6  B) 5  C) 4  D) 40  E) 8

**5**

$$38 + 35 = 90 - \boxed{?}$$

A) 87  B) 13  C) 17  D) 15  E) 16

**6**

$$65 \;-\; 30 \;=\; 90 \;-\; \boxed{?}$$

A 5　　　　B 43　　　　C 44　　　　D 55　　　　E 46

**7**

$$24 \;+\; 28 \;=\; 55 \;-\; \boxed{?}$$

A 1　　　　B 3　　　　C 0　　　　D 4　　　　E 52

**8**

$$36 \;=\; \boxed{?} \;\times\; 9$$

A 27　　　　B 3　　　　C 4　　　　D 5　　　　E 6

**9**

$$\boxed{?} \;=\; \blacklozenge \;+\; 57$$
$$\blacklozenge \;=\; 26$$

A 78　　　　B 83　　　　C 80　　　　D 81　　　　E 73

**10**

$$\boxed{?} \;=\; \blacklozenge \;\times\; 9$$
$$\blacklozenge \;=\; 7$$

A 16　　　　B 54　　　　C 57　　　　D 58　　　　E 63

**11**

$$\boxed{?} = \blacklozenge \div 2$$
$$\blacklozenge = 20$$

(A) 5     (B) 6     (C) 18     (D) 12     (E) 10

**12**

$$\boxed{?} = \blacklozenge \times 4$$
$$\blacklozenge = 12$$

(A) 36     (B) 40     (C) 44     (D) 48     (E) 50

**13**

$$\boxed{?} = \blacklozenge \div 3$$
$$\blacklozenge = 30$$

(A) 27     (B) 30     (C) 9     (D) 10     (E) 11

**14**

$$\boxed{?} = \blacklozenge + 24 - 19$$
$$\blacklozenge = 41$$

(A) 42     (B) 43     (C) 84     (D) 45     (E) 46

**15**

$$\boxed{?} = \blacklozenge + 30 + 45$$
$$\blacklozenge = 10$$

(A) 85     (B) 81     (C) 82     (D) 5     (E) 45

16

$\boxed{?}$ = ◆ – 34 – 15

◆ = 77

A 58      B 48      C 26      D 27      E 28

Directions: Which answer choice would complete the pattern?

**1**

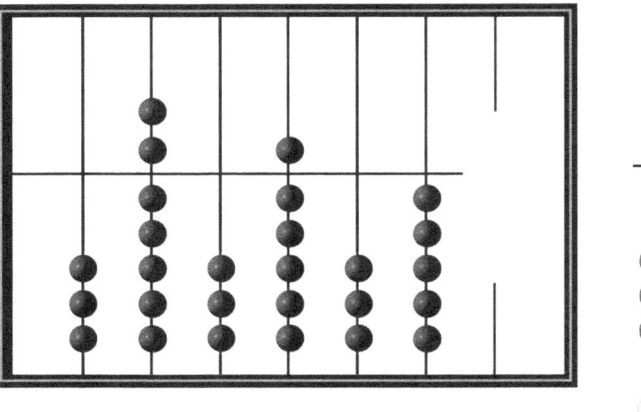 

A     B     C     D     E

**2**

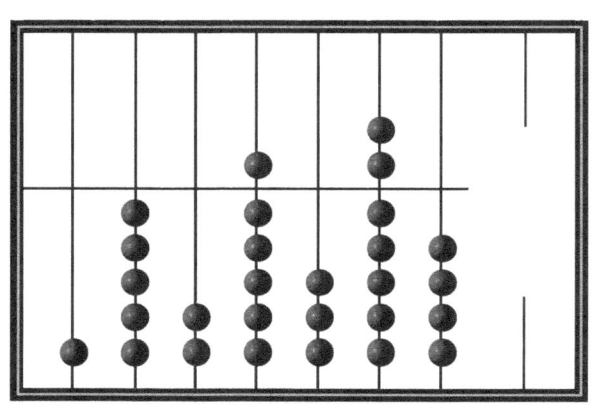  

A     B     C     D     E

**3**

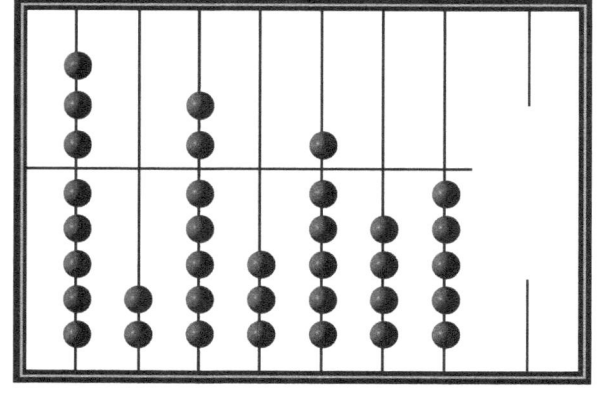   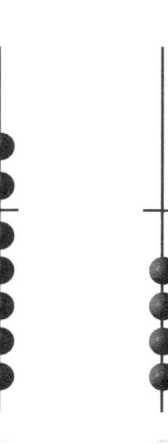

A     B     C     D     E

**4**

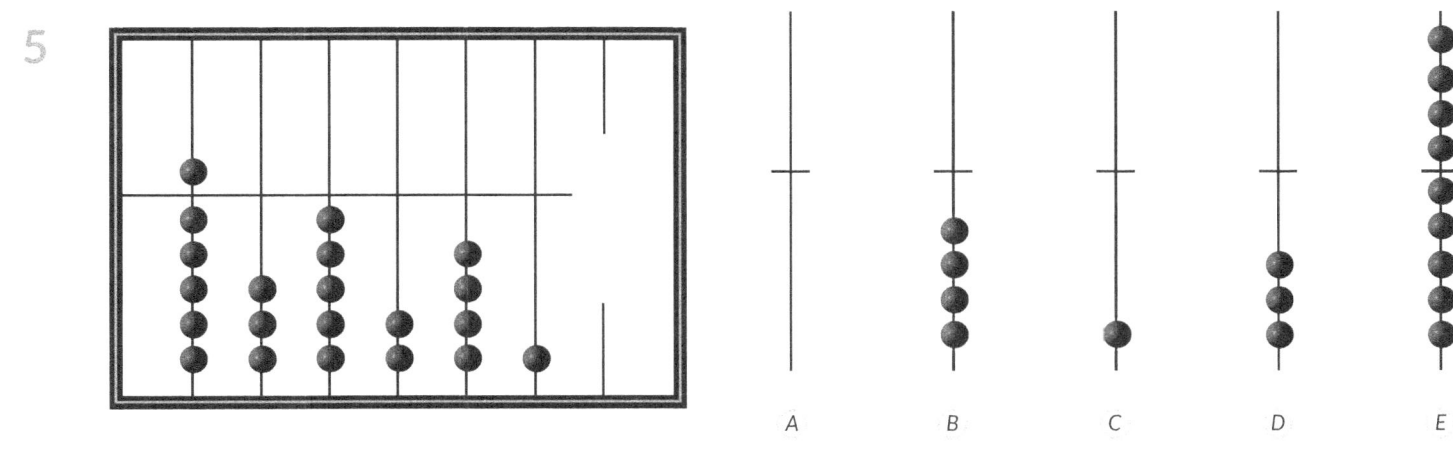

A B C D E

**5**

A B C D E

**6**

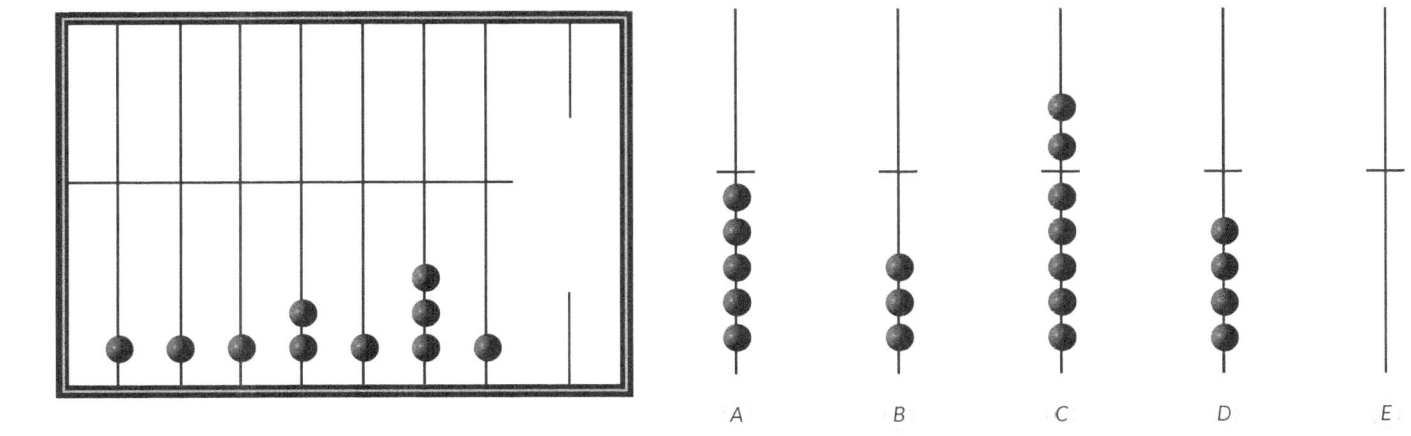

A B C D E

31

1.   **12**    **19**    **26**    **33**    **?**

    A 39    B 40    C 41    D 42    E 7

2.   **70**    **54**    **38**    **22**    **?**

    A 6    B 8    C 10    D 12    E 16

3.   **5**    **6**    **12**    **13**    **19**    **20**    **?**

    A 25    B 24    C 27    D 26    E 29

4.   **35**    **35**    **36**    **36**    **37**    **37**    **?**

    A 37    B 38    C 39    D 40    E 41

5.   **15**    **17**    **14**    **16**    **13**    **15**    **?**

    A 10    B 11    C 12    D 13    E 14

6.   **7**    **10**    **10**    **13**    **13**    **16**    **?**

    A 20    B 19    C 18    D 17    E 16

**7**  15   14   13   11   10   9   7   ?

A  9   B  8   C  7   D  6   E  5

**8**  19.2   16.2   13.2   10.2   7.2   4.2   ?

A  1.2   B  2.2   C  3.2   D  0.2   E  -1.2

**9**  3   4   5   7   8   9   11   12   ?

A  13   B  14   C  15   D  16   E  17

**10**  0   6   0   7   0   8   0   9   ?

A  9   B  0   C  11   D  10   E  13

**11**  0.04   0.06   0.08   0.10   0.12   0.14   ?

A  0.02   B  0.18   C  0.15   D  0.16   E  0.13

**12**  50   41   34   25   18   9   ?

A  0   B  1   C  2   D  3   E  4

# NUMBER ANALOGIES

**Directions:** The first set and second set of numbers go together in some way. Both of these sets must go together in the <u>same</u> way. Look at the third set where there is a question mark. What number should go here so that all three sets of numbers go together in the same way?

**1**

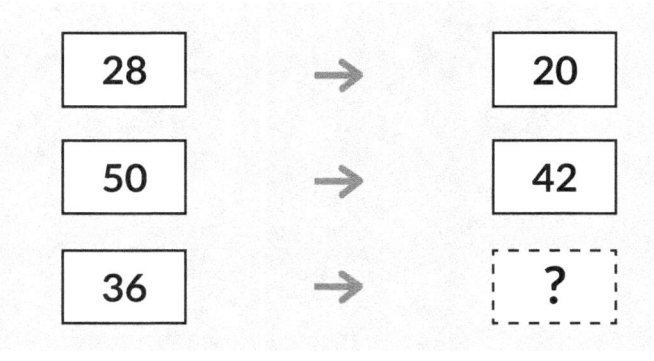

A. 26    B. 28    C. 30    D. 32    E. 34

**2**

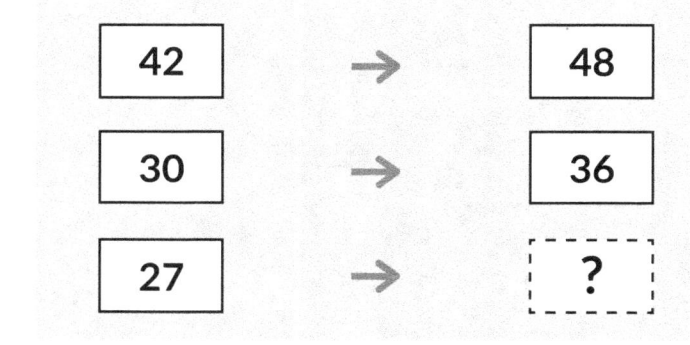

A. 29    B. 30    C. 31    D. 32    E. 33

**3**

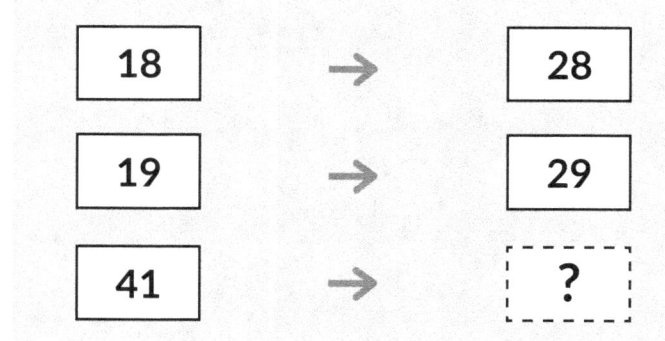

A. 49    B. 50    C. 51    D. 52    E. 53

**4**

| | | |
|---|---|---|
| 10 | → | 20 |
| 7 | → | 14 |
| 15 | → | ? |

A  25          B  22          C  30          D  31          E  32

**5**

| | | |
|---|---|---|
| 5 | → | 20 |
| 2 | → | 8 |
| 3 | → | ? |

A  4          B  7          C  9          D  12          E  18

**6**

| | | |
|---|---|---|
| 40 | → | 10 |
| 32 | → | 8 |
| 24 | → | ? |

A  6          B  4          C  28          D  0          E  14

**7**   [8 → 16]      [11 → 19]      [48 → ?]

   (A) 54     (B) 55     (C) 56     (D) 8     (E) 96

**8**   [4 → 2]      [60 → 58]      [34 → ?]

   (A) 30     (B) 32     (C) 17     (D) 33     (E) 34

**9**   [30 → 24]      [12 → 6]      [18 → ?]

   (A) 10     (B) 11     (C) 9     (D) 16     (E) 12

**10**   [3 → 6]      [30 → 33]      [21 → ?]

   (A) 42     (B) 23     (C) 24     (D) 30     (E) 22

**11**   [17 → 13]      [50 → 46]      [7 → ?]

   (A) 2     (B) 3     (C) 4     (D) 5     (E) 6

**12**   [48 → 38]      [33 → 23]      [55 → ?]

   (A) 35     (B) 36     (C) 65     (D) 45     (E) 60

13    [9  →  18]        [20  →  29]        [45  →  ?]

   A 54          B 49          C 50          D 55          E 90


14    [49  →  51]        [6  →  8]        [35  →  ?]

   A 38          B 37          C 32          D 39          E 42


15    [50  →  5]        [40  →  4]        [20  →  ?]

   A 20          B 22          C 3          D 4          E 2


16    [7  →  21]        [9  →  27]        [4  →  ?]

   A 22          B 11          C 18          D 12          E 3


17    [5  →  1]        [30  →  6]        [50  →  ?]

   A 8          B 9          C 10          D 15          E 5


18    [55  →  11]        [25  →  5]        [10  →  ?]

   A 2          B 5          C 15          D 11          E 0

# COGAT® PRACTICE TEST 3

# NUMBER PUZZLES

**Directions:** Which number would go in place of the question mark so that both of sides of the equal sign (point to the equal sign) have the same amount?

**1**      **75**   **=**   **?**   **+**   **42**

A  117         B  31         C  32         D  30         E  33

**2**      **55**   **=**   **72**   **–**   **?**

A  17         B  16         C  127         D  18         E  19

**3**      **48**   **÷**   **?**   **=**   **6**

A  6         B  7         C  8         D  9         E  42

**4**      **7**   **×**   **?**   **=**   **56**

A  5         B  6         C  7         D  8         E  49

**5**      **40**   **+**   **38**   **=**   **90**   **–**   **?**

A  12         B  88         C  78         D  15         E  16

**6**

$$65 - 35 = 85 - \boxed{?}$$

A. 15  B. 13  C. 55  D. 30  E. 16

**7**

$$32 + 20 = 60 - \boxed{?}$$

A. 5  B. 52  C. 7  D. 8  E. 48

**8**

$$42 = \boxed{?} \times 7$$

A. 5  B. 6  C. 7  D. 8  E. 35

**9**

$$\boxed{?} = \blacklozenge + 50 + 20$$
$$\blacklozenge = 15$$

A. 85  B. 80  C. 82  D. 70  E. 45

**10**

$$\boxed{?} = \blacklozenge - 37 - 18$$
$$\blacklozenge = 92$$

A. 35  B. 36  C. 37  D. 73  E. 55

11
$$? = \blacklozenge + 45 + 22$$
$$\blacklozenge = 9$$

A 74          B 76          C 32          D 77          E 67

12
$$? = \blacklozenge - 52 - 11$$
$$\blacklozenge = 90$$

A 27          B 28          C 49          D 30          E 131

13
$$? = \blacklozenge \div 5$$
$$\blacklozenge = 35$$

A 4          B 5          C 6          D 7          E 30

14
$$? = \blacklozenge \times 6$$
$$\blacklozenge = 9$$

A 52          B 3          C 15          D 56          E 54

15
$$? = \blacklozenge \div 8$$
$$\blacklozenge = 64$$

A 56          B 7          C 8          D 9          E 72

16

$$\boxed{?} = \blacklozenge \times 3$$
$$\blacklozenge = 15$$

(A) 18　　　(B) 12　　　(C) 40　　　(D) 45　　　(E) 55

Good job!

Keep it up!

Caleb

# NUMBER SERIES

**1**

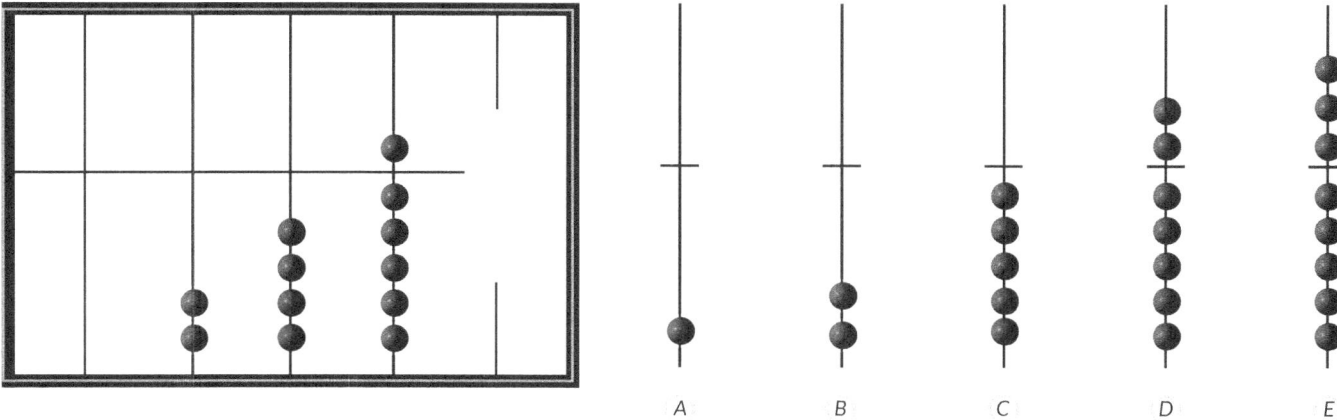

**2**

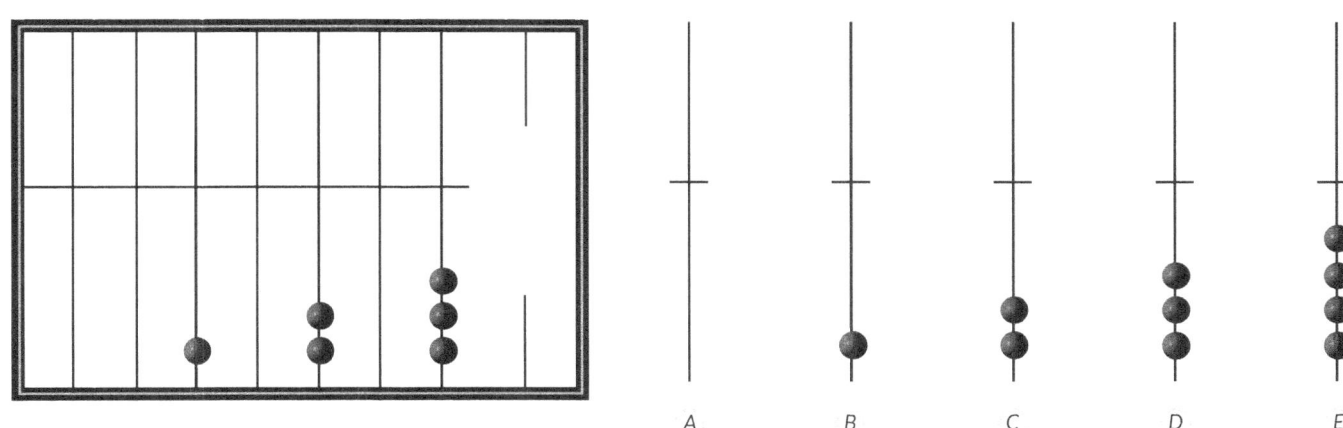

**3**

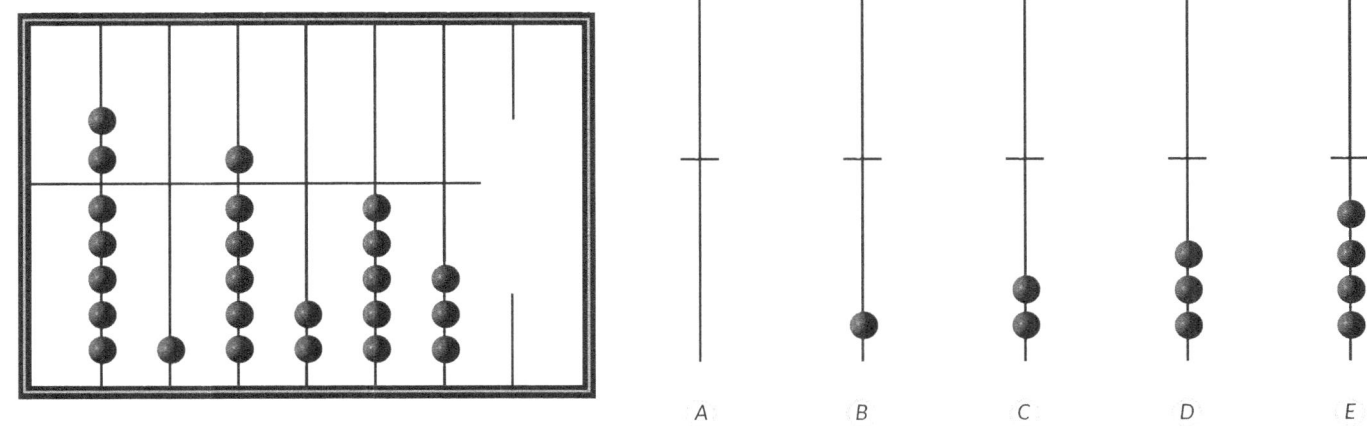

**4**

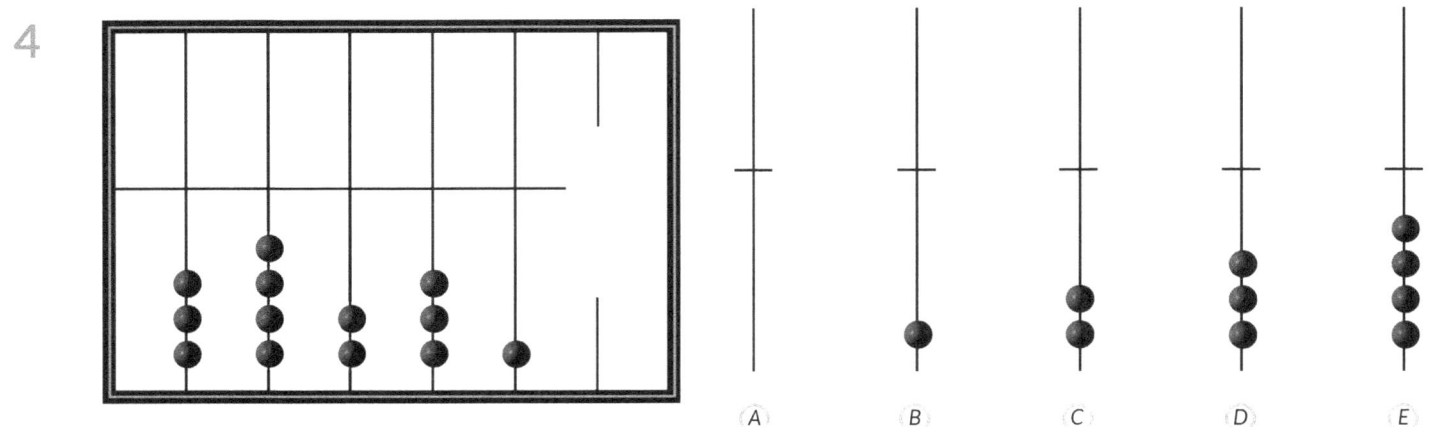

A     B     C     D     E

**5**

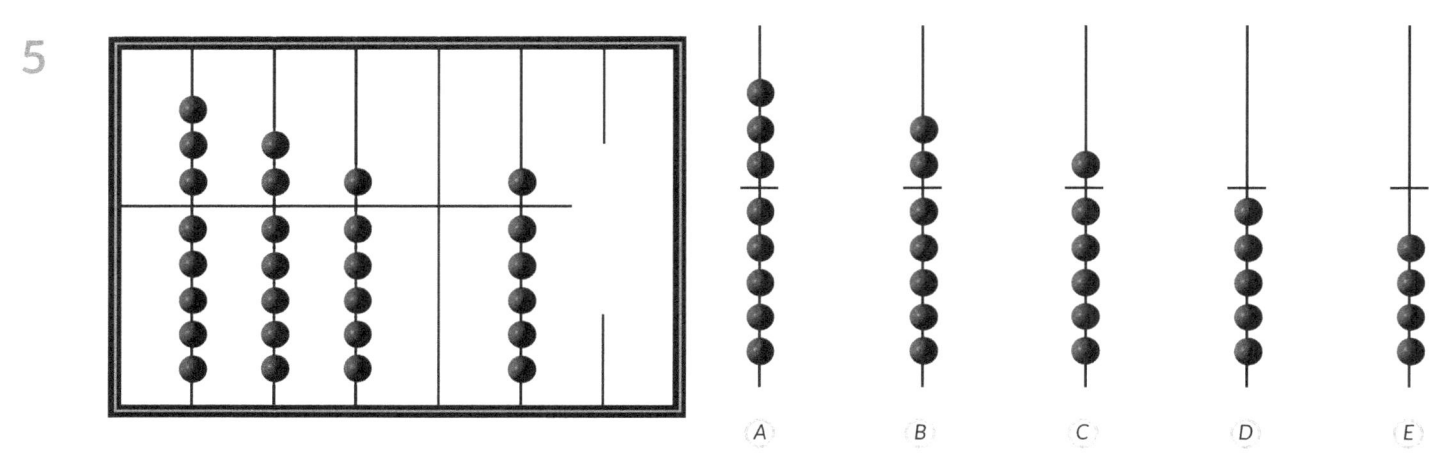

A     B     C     D     E

**6**

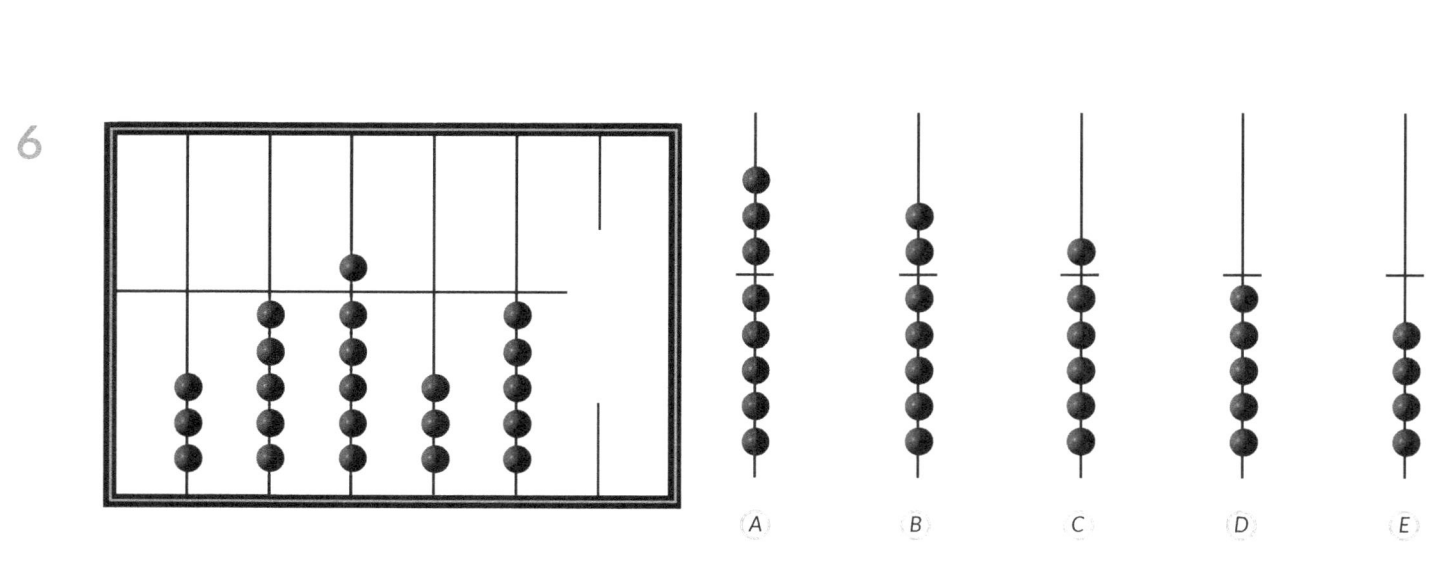

A     B     C     D     E

**1**

| 70 | 61 | 52 | 43 | 34 | 25 | ? |

A 16    B 17    C 18    D 19    E 20

**2**

| 19 | 22 | 23 | 26 | 27 | 30 | ? |

A 29    B 33    C 34    D 32    E 31

**3**

| 50 | 50 | 49 | 49 | 48 | ? |

A 47    B 46    C 45    D 44    E 48

**4**

| 10 | 0 | 9 | 0 | 8 | 0 | 7 | 0 | ? |

A 5    B 6    C 7    D 8    E 9

**5**

| 2.3 | 3.4 | 4.5 | 5.6 | 6.7 | 7.8 | ? |

A 8.8    B 9.1    C 9.0    D 8.9    E 9.2

**6**

| 12 | 22 | 26 | 36 | 40 | 50 | ? |

A 52    B 53    C 54    D 55    E 56

**7**   8   9   10   10   11   12   12   13   ?

Ⓐ 13   Ⓑ 14   Ⓒ 15   Ⓓ 16   Ⓔ 17

**8**   20   18   16   16   14   12   12   10   ?

Ⓐ 8   Ⓑ 9   Ⓒ 10   Ⓓ 11   Ⓔ 2

**9**   1   20   1   30   1   40   1   ?

Ⓐ 1   Ⓑ 10   Ⓒ 45   Ⓓ 50   Ⓔ 60

**10**   20   19   18   15   14   13   10   ?

Ⓐ 3   Ⓑ 6   Ⓒ 7   Ⓓ 8   Ⓔ 9

**11**   5   6   7   9   10   11   13   ?

Ⓐ 14   Ⓑ 15   Ⓒ 16   Ⓓ 17   Ⓔ 18

**12**   2   3   5   8   12   17   23   ?

Ⓐ 28   Ⓑ 29   Ⓒ 30   Ⓓ 31   Ⓔ 32

# NUMBER ANALOGIES

**Directions:** The first set and second set of numbers go together in some way. Both of these sets must go together in the <u>same</u> way. Look at the third set where there is a question mark. What number should go here so that all three sets of numbers go together in the same way?

1

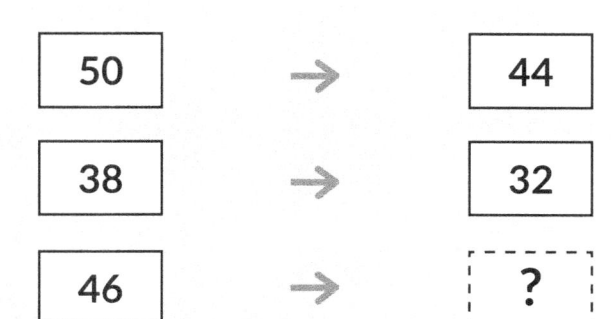

A 34     B 35     C 40     D 37     E 52

2

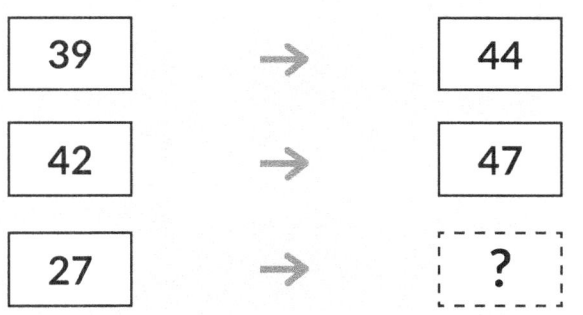

A 28     B 29     C 30     D 31     E 32

3

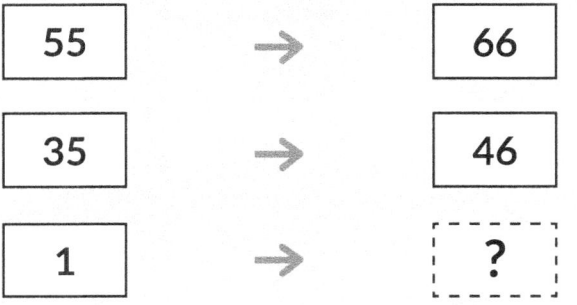

A 24     B 22     C 13     D 12     E 11

**4**

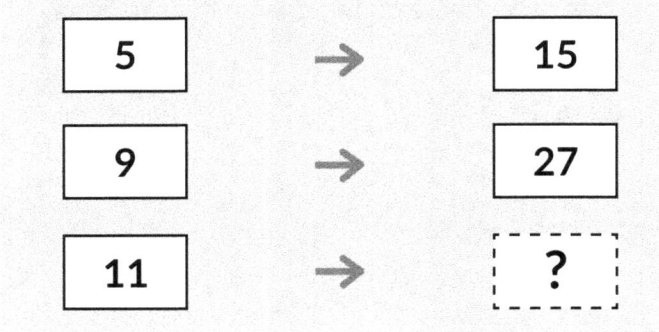

A 30     B 31     C 32     D 33     E 34

**5**

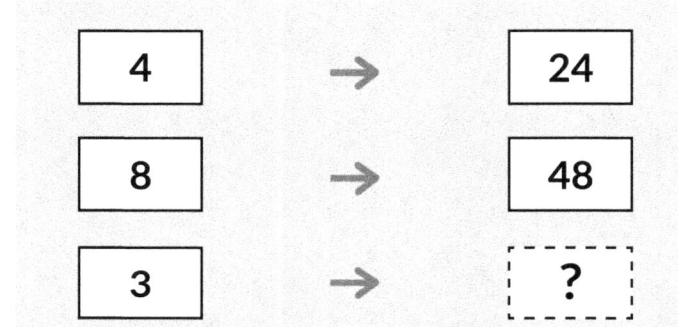

A 9     B 36     C 21     D 23     E 18

**6**

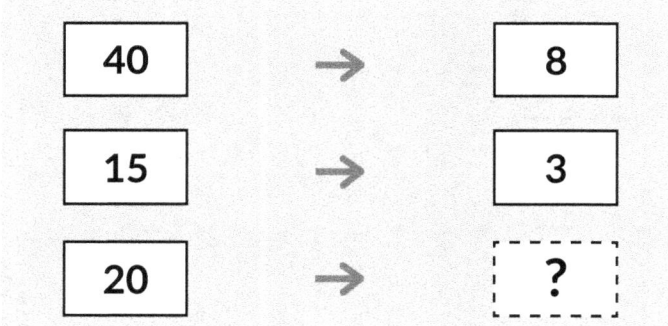

A 4     B 5     C 32     D 15     E 10

7   [44 → 53]        [20 → 29]        [61 → ?]

   A 60         B 67         C 68         D 69         E 70


8   [8 → 4]         [48 → 44]         [34 → ?]

   A 24         B 17         C 30         D 44         E 38


9   [50 → 39]        [22 → 11]        [11 → ?]

   A 0         B 1         C 10         D 5         E 6


10  [6 → 12]         [18 → 24]         [25 → ?]

   A 26         B 27         C 20         D 30         E 31


11  [30 → 24]        [54 → 48]         [18 → ?]

   A 10         B 8         C 16         D 12         E 14


12  [24 → 12]        [42 → 30]         [32 → ?]

   A 20         B 12         C 30         D 16         E 18

**13**  [38 → 46]    [1 → 9]    [8 → ?]

A 72     B 16     C 17     D 19     E 24

**14**  [20 → 10]    [16 → 8]    [10 → ?]

A 2     B 3     C 4     D 5     E 6

**15**  [20 → 2]    [100 → 10]    [80 → ?]

A 6     B 7     C 8     D 9     E 10

**16**  [6 → 24]    [8 → 32]    [7 → ?]

A 28     B 24     C 25     D 26     E 32

**17**  [55 → 11]    [20 → 4]    [0 → ?]

A 4     B 5     C 2     D 1     E 0

**18**  [21 → 3]    [35 → 5]    [56 → ?]

A 6     B 7     C 8     D 9     E 49

# ANSWER KEYS

# ANSWER KEY FOR PRACTICE TEST 1 (WORKBOOK FORMAT)

## Number Puzzles, Practice Test 1

1. C.
2. C.
3. B.
4. D.
5. A.
6. E.
7. D.
8. E.
9. B.
10. C.
11. A.
12. E.
13. D.
14. E.
15. A.
16. D.

## Number Series, Practice Test 1 - Abacus Format

1. A: every other rod has 0 -and- after that, every other rod decreases by 2 (7-5-3-1)

2. B: the pattern is: 4-5-6-7, 4-5-6-7

3. D: every other rod increases by 1 (1-2-3-4) -and- after that, every other rod has 7

4. B: every other rod increases by 1 (0-1-2-3) -and- after that, every other rod increases by 1 (5-6-7)

5. E: the pattern is: 6-3-5-2, 6-3-5-2

6. B: every other rod decreases by 1 (7-6-5-4) -and- after that, every other rod decreases by 1 (3-2-1)

7. D: the pattern is: 3-0-0, 3-0-0

## Number Series, Practice Test 1 - Number Format

8. C. +4
9. C. +1, +2, +1, +2, etc.
10. B. -1, -2, -1, -2, -1, etc.
11. E. +2, +3, +2, +3, etc.
12. A. +2, +0, +2, +0, etc.
13. D. -1, -1, -2, -1, -1, -2, etc.
14. E. +2
15. C. +7
16. E. +5, +10, +5, +10, etc.
17. C. +11, -6, +11, -6, etc.
18. A. +1, +1, +0, +1, +1, +0
19. D. -2, +1, -2, +1, -2, +1

## Number Analogies, Practice Test 1

1. B. subtract 1
2. C. multiply by 2
3. C. add 3
4. A. multiply by 4
5. E. subtract 5
6. D. divide by 3
7. A. divide by 10
8. C. add 9
9. E. divide by 2
10. B. subtract 8
11. C. subtract 6
12. D. add 8
13. E. subtract 12
14. A. multiply by 6
15. E. subtract 10
16. D. divide by 4
17. C. subtract 7
18. C. divide by 3

# ANSWER KEY FOR PRACTICE TEST 2

## Number Puzzles, Practice Test 2

1. B.
2. E.
3. C.
4. A.
5. C.
6. D.
7. B.
8. C.
9. B.
10. E.
11. E.
12. D.
13. D.
14. E.
15. A.
16. E.

## Number Series, Practice Test 2 - Abacus Format

1. A: every other rod has 3 -and- after that, every other rod decreases by 1 (7-6-5)

2. E: every other rod increases by 1 (1-2-3-4) -and- after that, every other rod increases by 1 (5-6-7-8)

3. A: every other rod decreases by 1 (8-7-6-5) -and- after that, every other rod increases by 1 (2-3-4-5)

4. C: 3-8-6-5, 3-8-6-5

5. D: every other rod decreases by 1 (6-5-4-3) -and- after that, every other rod decreases by 1 (3-2-1)

6. D: every other rod has 1 -and- after that, every other rod increases by 1 (1-2-3-4)

## Number Series, Practice Test 2 - Number Format

1. B. +7
2. A. -16
3. D. +1, +6, +1, +6, etc.
4. B. +0, +1, +0, +1, etc.
5. C. +2, -3, +2, -3, etc.
6. E. +3, +0, +3, +0, etc.
7. D. -1, -1, -2, -1, -1, -2, etc.
8. A. -3
9. A. +1, +1, +2, +1, +1, +2, etc.
10. B. every other number is 0 -and- after that, every other number increases by 1
11. D. +0.02
12. C. -9, -7, -9, -7, etc.


## Number Analogies, Practice Test 2

1. B. subtract 8
2. E. add 6
3. C. add 10
4. C. multiply by 2
5. D. multiply by 4
6. A. divide by 4
7. C. add 8
8. B. subtract 2
9. E. subtract 6
10. C. add 3
11. B. subtract 4
12. D. subtract 10
13. A. add 9
14. B. add 2
15. E. divide by 10
16. D. multiply by 3
17. C. divide by 5
18. A. divide by 5

# ANSWER KEY FOR PRACTICE TEST 3

## Number Puzzles, Practice Test 3

| | | | | | |
|---|---|---|---|---|---|
| 1. E. | 2. A. | 3. C. | 4. D. | 5. A. | 6. C. |
| 7. D. | 8. B. | 9. A. | 10. C. | 11. B. | 12. A. |
| 13. D. | 14. E. | 15. C. | 16. D. | | |

## Number Series, Practice Test 3 - Abacus Format

1. E: each rod increases by 2
2. A: every other rod is 0 -and- after that, every other rod increases by 1 (0-1-2-3)
3. E: every other rod decreases by 1 (7-6-5-4) -and- after that, every other rod increases by 1 (1-2-3)
4. C: every other rod decreases by 1 (3-2-1) -and- after that, every other rod decreases by 1 (4-3-2)
5. B: the pattern decreases until it gets to zero, then reverses and begins to increase: 8-7-6-0-6-7
6. C: the pattern is 3-5-6, 3-5-6

## Number Series, Practice Test 3 - Number Format

1. A. -9
2. E. +3, +1, +3, +1, etc.
3. E. -0, -1, -0, -1, etc.
4. B. every other number is 0 -and- after that, every other number decreases by 1
5. D. +1.1
6. C. +10, +4, +10, +4, etc.
7. B. +1, +1, +0, +1, +1, +0, +1, +1
8. A. -2, -2, -0, -2, -2, -0, -2, -2
9. D. every other number is one -and- after that, 10 is added to every other number
10. E. -1, -1, -3, -1, -1, -3, -1
11. A. +1, +1, +2, +1, +1, +2, +1
12. C. +1, +2, +3, +4, +5, +6, +7

**Number Analogies, Practice Test 3**

1. C. subtract 6
2. E. add 5
3. D. add 11
4. D. multiply by 3
5. E. multiply by 6
6. A. divide by 5
7. E. add 9
8. C. subtract 4
9. A. subtract 11
10. E. add 6
11. D. subtract 6
12. A. subtract 12
13. B. add 8
14. D. divide by 2
15. C. divide by 10
16. A. multiply by 4
17. E. divide by 5
18. C. divide by 7

## READY FOR TEST DAY?

• Get 300+ <u>new</u> questions per book.

• Check out Savant Test Prep™ books on Amazon®.